THE LIFE OF
SAINT MARY OF EGYPT

Revised by

St. Mary and St. Moses Abbey

ST Mary & Moses

ABBEY PRESS

The Life of Saint Mary of Egypt

Revised by St. Mary & St. Moses Abbey.

Cover design by St. Mary & St. Moses Abbey.

Designed & Published by:
St. Mary & St. Moses Abbey Press
101 S Vista Dr, Sandia, TX 78383
stmabbeypress.com

Contents

The Story of Abba Zosimus

In the reign of Theodosius the Younger, there lived in Palestine, a holy monk and priest named Zosimus, famed for the reputation of his sanctity, and was known as one who knew the direction of souls in the most perfect rules of a religious life. He had served God from his youth with great fervor, in the same house, for the space of 53 years, when he was tempted to think that he had attained to a state of perfection, and that no one could teach him anything more in regard to the monastic life. To discover the delusion and danger of this suggestion of the proud spirit, and to convince him that we may always advance in perfection, God directed him by revelation to quit his monastery for one near the Jordan, where he might learn lessons of virtue he yet was unacquainted with. Being admitted among them, it was not long before he was undeceived, and convinced, from what he saw practiced there, how much he had been mistaken in the judgment he had formed of himself and his advancement in virtue. The members of this community had no more communication with the rest of mankind, than if they had belonged to another world. The whole employment of their lives was manual labor, which they accompanied with prayer, and the singing of psalms, (in which heavenly exercise they spent the whole night, relieving each other by turns), and their chief sustenance was bread and water. It was their yearly custom, after having assisted at the divine mysteries, and receiving the blessed Eucharist on the first Sunday in Great Fast, to cross the river, and disperse themselves over the vast deserts which lie towards Arabia, to pass in perfect solitude the interval [of time] between that and Palm-Sunday; at which time they all returned again to the monastery to join in celebrating the passion and resurrection of our Lord. Some subsisted during this time on a small parcel of provision they took with them, while others lived on the herbs which grew wild; but when they came back, they never communicated to each other what they did during that time.

Abba Zosimus Meets St. Mary of Egypt

One year, the holy man Zosimus passed over the Jordan with the rest at the usual time, praying with great fervor as he traveled, endeavoring to penetrate as far as he could into the wilderness, in hopes of meeting with some hermit of greater perfection than he had seen or conversed with. Having advanced thus for twenty days, as he one day stopped at noon to rest himself and recite a certain number of psalms, according to custom, he saw as it were the figure of a human body. He was at first seized with fright and astonishment; and imagining it might be an illusion of the enemy, he armed himself with the sign of the cross and continued in prayer.

Having finished his devotions, he plainly perceived, on turning his eyes that way, that it was somebody that appeared naked, extremely sunburnt, and with short white hair, who walked very quick, and fled from him. Zosimus, judging it was some holy anchorite, ran that way with all his speed to overtake him. He drew nearer by degrees, and when he was within hearing distance, he cried out to the person to stop and bless him; who answered: "Abbot Zosimus, I am a woman; throw me your mantle to cover me, so that you may come near me." He, surprised to hear her call him by his name, which he was convinced she could have known only by revelation, readily complied with her request. Having covered herself with his garment she approached him, and they entered into conversation after mutual prayer.

Her Early Life

And on the holy man's conjuring her by Jesus Christ to tell him who she was, how long, and in what manner she had lived in that desert, she said, "I ought to die with confusion and shame in telling you what I am; so horrible is the very mention of it, that you will fly from me as from a serpent: your ears will not be able to bear the recital of the crimes of which I have been guilty. I will however relate to you my disgrace begging of you to pray for me, that God may show me mercy in the day of His dreadful judgment.

"My country is Egypt. When my father and mother were still living, at twelve years of age I went without their consent to Alexandria: I cannot think, without trembling, on the first steps by which I fell into sin, nor my disorders which followed."

She then described how she lived as a public prostitute for seventeen years, not for interest, but to gratify an unbridled lust. She added, "I continued my wicked course till the twenty-ninth year of my age, when, perceiving several persons making towards the sea, I inquired where they were going, and was told they were about to embark for the holy land, to celebrate in Jerusalem the feast of the Exaltation of the glorious Cross of our Savior. I embarked with them, looking only for fresh opportunities to continue my corruption, which I repeated both during the voyage and after my arrival at Jerusalem.

Her Conversion

On the day appointed for the feast, all going to church, I mixed with the crowd to get into the church where the holy cross was shown and exposed to the veneration of the faithful; however, I found myself withheld from entering the place by some secret and invisible force. This happened to me three or four times. I retired into a corner of the courtyard, and began to consider with myself what this might proceed from; and seriously reflecting that my criminal life might be the cause, I melted into tears. Beating therefore my sinful breast, with sighs and groans, I perceived above me a picture of the Mother of God.

"Fixing my eyes upon it, I addressed myself to that

holy Virgin, begging of her, by her incomparable purity, to rescue me, defiled with such a load of abominations, and to render my repentance the more acceptable to God. I beseeched her that I might be allowed to enter the church doors to behold the sacred wood of my redemption, promising from that moment to consecrate myself to God by a life of repentance, taking her for my surety in this change of my heart. After this ardent prayer, I perceived in my soul a secret consolation under my grief; and attempting again to enter the church, I went up with ease into the very middle of it, and had the comfort to venerate the precious wood of the glorious cross which brings life to man.

"Considering therefore the incomprehensible mercy of God, and His readiness to receive sinners to repentance, I cast myself on the ground, and after having kissed the pavement with tears, I arose and went to the picture of the Mother of God, whom I had made the witness and surety of my engagements and resolutions. Falling there on my knees before her image, I addressed my prayers to her, begging for her intercession, and that she would be my guide. After my prayer, I seemed to hear this voice: 'If you go beyond the Jordan, you shall find there rest and comfort.'"

Renouncing the World

"Weeping and looking on the image, I begged the holy

queen of the world that she would never abandon me. After these words, I went out in haste, bought three loaves, and asking the baker which was gate of the city which led to the Jordan, I immediately took that road, and walked all the rest of the day, and at night arrived at the church of St. John Baptist on the banks of the river. There I paid my devotions to God, and received the precious body of our Savior Jesus Christ. Having ate the half of one of my loaves, I slept all night on the ground. Next morning, endorsing myself to the holy Virgin, I passed the Jordan, and from that time I have carefully shunned the meeting of any human creature."

Her Life in the Desert

Zosimus asked how long she had lived in that desert. "It is, as near as I can judge, forty-seven years." "And what have you subsisted upon all that time?" replied Zosimus. "The loaves I took with me lasted me some time. Since then I have had no other food but what this wild and uncultivated solitude afforded me. My clothes being worn out, I suffered severely from the heat and the cold, with which I was often so afflicted that I was not able to stand."

"And have you passed so many years," said the holy man, "without suffering much in your soul?"

She answered: "Your question makes me tremble, by the very remembrance of my past dangers and conflicts, through the perverseness of my heart. Seventeen years I passed in most violent temptations, and never-ending conflicts with my inordinate desires. I was tempted to regret the flesh and fish of Egypt, and the wines which I drank in the world to excess; whereas here I often could not come at a drop of water to quench my thirst. Other desires made assaults on my mind; but, weeping and striking my breast on those occasions, I called to mind the vows I had made under the protection of the Blessed Virgin, and begged her to obtain my deliverance from the affliction and danger of such thoughts. After long weeping and bruising my body with blows, I found myself suddenly enlightened and my mind restored to a perfect calm. Often the tyranny of my old passions seemed ready to drag me out of my desert. At those times I threw myself on the ground and watered it with my tears, raising my heart continually to the Blessed Virgin till she secured me with comfort. And she has never failed to show herself as my faithful protectress."

Zosimus taking notice that in her discourse with him she from time to time made use of scripture phrases, asked her if she had ever applied herself to the study of the sacred books. Her answer was that she could not even read, neither had she conversed nor seen any human creature since she came into the desert till that day, that could teach her to read the holy scripture or read it to her. But, she said, "It is God that teaches man knowledge. Now that I have given you a full account of myself, keep what I have told you as an inviolable secret during my life, and allow me, the most miserable of sinners, a share in your prayers."

She concluded with desiring him not to pass over the Jordan next Great Fast, according to the custom of his monastery, but to bring with him on Covenant Thursday the body and blood of our Lord, and wait for her on the banks of the river on the side which is inhabited. Having spoken thus, and once more entreated him to pray for her, she left him. Zosimus immediately then fell on his knees, thanked God for what he had seen and heard, kissed the ground whereon she had stood, and returned by the usual time to his monastery.

St. Mary Partakes of the Eucharist

The following year, on the first Sunday of Great Fast, he was detained at home on account of sickness, as indeed she had foretold him. On Covenant Thursday, taking the sacred body and blood of our Lord in a small chalice, and also a little basket of figs, dates, and lentils, he went to the banks of the Jordan. At night she appeared on the other side, and making the sign of the cross over the river, she went forward, walking upon the surface of the water, as if it had been dry land, till she reached the opposite shore. Being now together, she craved his blessing, and desired him to recite the Creed and the Lord's Prayer, after which she received from his hands the holy Eucharist. Then lifting up her hands to heaven, she said aloud with tears: Now you may dismiss your servant, O Lord, according to your word, in peace; because my eyes have seen my Savior. She begged Zosimus to pardon the trouble she had given him, and desired him to return the following Great Fast, to the place where he first saw her. He begged of her to accept the sustenance he had brought her, but she took only a few of the lentils; and conjuring him never to forget her miseries, left him, and then went over the river as she came.

St. Mary's Departure

Zosimus returned home, and at the very time fixed by the saint, set out in quest of her, with the view of being still further edified by holy conversation, and of learning also her name, which he had forgot to ask. But on his arrival at the place where he had first seen her, he found her corpse stretched out on the ground, with an inscription declaring her name, Mary, and the time of her death, which was a year before, on the very night on which he had given her Holy Communion. Zosimus, being miraculously assisted by a lion, dug a grave, and buried her. Having recommended both himself and the whole church to the saint's intercession, he returned to his monastery, where he recounted all that he had seen and heard of this holy repentant, and continued there to serve God till his happy death, which happened in the hundredth year of his age. It is from a relation of the monks of that community, that an author of the same century, not very long after her death, wrote her life as above related, which history is mentioned soon after by many authors, both of the Eastern and Western church. Her death is dated to be in AD 421 at the age of 77.

Exhortation

In the example of this holy woman, we admire the wonderful goodness and mercy of God, who raised her from the pit of the most criminal habits and the most abandoned state, to the most sublime and heroic virtue. While we consider her severe repentance, let us be embarrassed in the manner in which we pretend to be repentant. Let her example rouse our sloth. The kingdom of heaven is only for those who do violence to themselves [in ascetic works]. Let us tremble with her at the remembrance of our baseness and sins, as often as we enter the sanctuary of the Lord or venerate His holy cross, the instrument of our redemption. We insult Him when we pretend exteriorly to give Him honor, and at the same time dishonor Him by our sloth and sinful life. God, by the miraculous visible rejection of this sinner in the church, shows us what He does invisibly with regard to all obstinate willful sinners. We join the crowd of adorers at the foot of His altar; but He abhors our treacherous kisses like those of Judas. We honor His cross with our lips, but He sees our heart, and condemns its inconsistencies and opposition to His Holy Spirit of perfect humility, meekness, self- denial, and charity. Shall we then so much fear to provoke His indignation by our unworthiness, as to keep at a distance from His holy places or mysteries? Absolutely not. This would lead to damnation, by cutting off the most essential means of salvation.

We are invited by the infinite goodness and mercy of God, but are pressed by our own sins and desires, which the more dangerous they are, need to have much greater earnestness and diligence to plead for pardon and grace, provided we do this in the most profound sentiments of compunction, fear, and confidence. It will be beneficial to often pray with the publican at a distance from the altar, in a feeling that we should be treated as persons who are excommunicated before God and men. Sometimes we may, in public prayers, pronounce the words with a lower voice, as unworthy to unite our praises with others. We are as base sinners, whose worshipping ought rather to be offensive to God and He hates the sight of a heart filled with iniquity and self-love. We must at least never present ourselves before God without purifying our hearts by compunction, and trembling, to say to ourselves, that God ought to drive us out of His holy presence with a voice of thunder. But in these dispositions of fear and humility, we must not fail to diligently pour forth our supplications, and sound the divine praises with our whole hearts.

Doxology for St. Mary of Egypt

(6th of Parmoute \ 14th of April)

Blessed are you truly, O Saint Mary of Egypt, the Bride of Christ, the pure Bridegroom.

For you have forsaken the glory of this world and the pride of this age, for you loved Christ.

For truly it is great, the chosen struggle of Saint Mary of Egypt, full of holiness.

She completed her life with great humility, and reposed with the saints in the region of the living.

Hail to the holy ascetic; hail to the truly chosen; hail to the Bride of Christ, Saint Mary of Egypt.

Pray to the Lord on our behalf, O Bride of Christ, Saint Mary of Egypt, that He may forgive us our sins.

Veneration for St. Mary of Egypt

(6ᵗʰ of Parmoute \ 14ᵗʰ of April)

I start, my brethren, to move my tongue, to glorify
faithfully,

Mary of Egypt

This pure one, born in Alexandria, into Christian family.

Mary of Egypt

When she turned peacefully twelve years old, the
reproached enemy deceived her.

Mary of Egypt

Through her the devil hunted many souls, O my
brethren; she was boldly living in impurity.

Mary of Egypt

She remained in that state, living an unruly life, for
seventeen years,

Mary of Egypt

Until the love of her Creator called upon her, and one
day she saw

Mary of Egypt

People who were travelling to Jerusalem; she went with
them certainly.

Mary of Egypt

As she had no fare for her trip, so she gave herself

Mary of Egypt

To those on the ship with a cursed soul, and she reached the port.

Mary of Egypt

When she wanted to enter, with acceptance, to the church, she felt the hand of the Awesome

Mary of Egypt

Drawing her back; so, O my beloved, she felt this to be a punishment for her acts

Mary of Egypt

Due to her unchastity and her severe defilement. So she lifted up her eyes to her Creator,

Mary of Egypt

With a contrite heart, and wept with love, asking for the intercession of the Mother of the Lord.

Mary of Egypt

She asked her with tears, to intercede for her before Jesus, as her voice is heard by Him.

Mary of Egypt

The chaste one gained courage and desired to enter, so she found acceptance.

Mary of Egypt

She entered, O you who are present; she worshipped with the worshippers and prayed in faith.

Mary of Egypt

She asked God to guide her to what pleases Him and to take His anger away from her.

Mary of Egypt

She gained support and stood before the icon of the compassionate Virgin.

Mary of Egypt

She asked her fervently to guide her with wisdom to a life of piety,

Mary of Egypt

To the place of her salvation, so she heard a voice telling her, "You will find it in the Jordan."

Mary of Egypt

So she arose at once, and on her way, she met a man who gave her,

Mary of Egypt

Three dirhams of silver, with which she bought three loaves.

Mary of Egypt

She crossed the Jordan River, and remained in the desert, for forty-seven years.

Mary of Egypt

She met Abba Zosimus, who gave her Communion; then she departed.

Mary of Egypt

The father saw next to her a lion watching over her, and above her was written,

Mary of Egypt

"O Zosimus, my father, bury the poor one, Mary the faithful."

Mary of Egypt

He prayed to his Lord for her and buried her with his hands, and returned to his monastery.

Mary of Egypt

May her prayers be with us; she carries our requests to the Lord, that He may accept us.

Mary of Egypt

Let her be a guard to us against conspiracies, that we may inherit the kingdom.

Mary of Egypt

O you, the one beloved by God, we say to you, "Worthy, worthy, worthy."

Mary of Egypt

The mention of Your name is in all the believers' mouths. They all say, "O God of St. Mary of Egypt, help all of us!"

About the Text

The following sources were used to produce this revised Life of St. Mary of Egypt. The first reference is the main source which was revised using the second and third references:

✤ *The Lives of the Primitive Fathers, Martyrs, and Other Principal Saints* 4, A. Butler, ed. (Edinburgh, UK: J. Moir, 1798), 88–95.

✤ *The Catholic Encyclopedia* 9, C.G. Herbermann, E.A. Pace, C.B. Pallen, T.J. Shahan, and J.J. Wynne, eds. (New York, NY: Robert Appleton Company, 1910), 763–764.

✤ Coptic Synaxarion, Parmoute 6.

Archaic English words were replaced by equivalent modern English words, to enhance readability and meaning.

The doxology and veneration were retrieved and slightly revised from The Coptic Orthodox Diocese of the Southern United States. *Coptic Reader* (2.97) [Mobile app]. App Store. https://apps.apple.com/us/app/coptic-reader/id649434138?ign-mpt=uo%3D4.

www.ingramcontent.com/pod-product-compliance
Lightning Source LLC
Chambersburg PA
CBHW030014040426
42337CB00012BA/777